A LATE FLOWERING

David Clarke

Also by David Clarke

Insight Through English (2 vols.)

The Language of Literature

Powers of Expression

Plays for Children

The River-Witch

The Down-Going of Orpheus Hawkins

A LATE FLOWERING

David Clarke

HIPPOPOTAMUS PRESS

ACKNOWLEDGEMENTS are due to the editors of the following magazines: *Acumen, Agenda, Envoi, The Frogmore Papers, Iota, Lines Review, Martin Holroyd's Poetry Monthly, Orbis, Ore, Other Poetry, Outposts Poetry Quarterly, Pennine Platform, Poetry Nottingham, Poetry Now, Seam, Smiths Knoll, Staple, Tears in the Fence, Weyfarers.*

In Memory of Philip Larkin won first prize in the 1993 Open University National Poetry Competition.

First published in 1997 by
HIPPOPOTAMUS PRESS
22, Whitewell Road,
Frome, Somerset, BA11 4EL

ISBN 0 904179 64 8

British Library Cataloguing in Publication Data

A Catalogue record for this book is available
from the British Library

Ten copies only have been numbered and signed by the author

Cover photograph of *Echinops bannaticus* by Simon Clarke

Printed in Great Britain by Latimer Trend & Company Ltd.
Plymouth, Devon

For My Dear Wife

Susan

with love and gratitude

CONTENTS

WALKING WITH HER

We both love the evening peace,
that line of poplars, the elm,
this sweep of lawn, but none of it
cares for us. Our pleasure is
the price we pay for being here,
our rent.

            All these paths
lead to loss, my love, and when
one of us goes, the other
will only know the wind will
settle for desolation,
unlike the stadium's roar before
it reaches the evening news
in a humped, dark town.

CAMPBELL ON CONISTON WATER
4th January, 1967

This boat has one main purpose: thrust.
      He turns its blue
and elegant, enormous power, just
after dawn, to face the lake again. What will ensue
is a matter for prayer, since no engineer
can tinker with time: the dead-line
is drawn on the water. Last weather checks are done,
all technicalities complete. On the mere
machinery growls and throbs, till at a sign
the lake gets ready for the second run.

Far off, a hum tinges the morning's void.
      Look! It's alive—
a blue flash, whining, paranoid,
its graceful spray streaming like a Saturn 5
rocket. The boat screams under compulsion
of engine and ancestry and is set
on course for devastation, as the roar
rips through the hills' wild applause. Propulsion
like this is uplifting! Jets
of water craze the lake; the boat bounces, soars—

(Thrilled, at first, watching the boat accelerate,
      I guessed the man's
motive was money or a need to emulate
his father. It was easy to call his plans
pointless or reckless, or mad, but debt
and misery drove him to shout *I can't hold on!*
as did the wheel, and when he cried
over the crackling radio *I'm going*, he met
death too fast to declare his next intention.)

—flips in the air like a high, bright plume,
        then curves and swoops
through fountains of exploding spume
to smash in the water. Startled groups
stare—mice, herons, voles—before they resume
their own affairs. Silence drifts on
into the trees. Obliteration now provides
the head-lines in each earnest city
where shrill phones ring. A single swan,
once the water's rocking chop and slap subsides,
patrols the lake's immense serenity.

Donald Campbell (1921-1967) at one time held the world land speed record
and the world water speed record. He raised the world water speed record
many times. On 4th January, 1967 he reached a speed of 527.86 km/h on
Coniston Water minutes before he was killed.

PHOTOGRAPH OF AN INFANT CLASS

Like flowers in a jug their faces
bloom, the picture faded, scuffed around the edge.
Pigtailed and sinless little girls
and grubby boys watch the important birdie
from a world where *Rover has the ball*
and days are sunny or end in tears.

No use guessing what grand careers,
weddings or wealth these tiny lives
grew into, or whether they failed
in the usual ways: illness
and unemployment and despair.
They're all dead now. Yet here, unfashionable,
they remain and have just been told
to be still for a moment and are,
as if their teacher believed she could water them so
and they'd flourish, despite the fact that she'd know
the school and its treasured playground swing
round the sun through pitiless solar winds.

IN MEMORY OF PHILIP LARKIN
for Anthony Thwaite

He was at odds with life, perplexed
(from 1940 when his letters start
to 1985 when he departs)
and hurt by everything from sex
to politics. He didn't like
most poets, immigrants, or strikes

or unions or marriage or the French,
found quitting Belfast something of a wrench,
always complained about the price of booze
and petrol and the loss of privacy
and smarmy social meetings; so he chose
a haven in pornography

and jazz. Sentenced to Hull for thirty years,
he strolled about his library and swore
he hated work, found writing poems a chore,
and, terrified of death, preferred
to steer towards these less poetic ends:
gossip, contracts, holding on to friends.

Yet this deaf hypochondriac,
who felt a fraud when poems died, inspired
a loyalty that others lack.
A troubled man; his friends admired
his mockery of self, his wry
malicious wit, his nature shy

and sensitive. They also knew the pain
his being irredeemably alone
caused him from first to last. The strain
of getting nearer now to the unknown
shows in his letters, though he tried to laugh.
Let that bleak vision be his epitaph.

FATHER AND SON

He thought that economic ties would bind
his wayward son, make him obedient,
and so he drew attention to the vast
inheritance success as architect
had brought him. This, he said, would be his son's,
provided he obeyed; such massive wealth
the legacy of sound investment bonds
and smart transactions on the Stock Exchange.

Now more than ever need to follow rules.
His scheme, escape by air, was dangerous;
extortionate the cost in coin and lives
of smuggled wax and powerful feathering
to fashion means to lift them from the maze
that he once built to hold the Minotaur.
The creature slouched its lanes and spent long days
watching the sun, hearing the warm sea wash,
scenting its human food, tasting the blood.

Nevertheless the project went ahead
with whispered calculations, new designs,
shift-work and trials. When at last they rose
above the puzzle and its predator
howling and gazing skywards, far beyond
that place of sacrifice and pain they spied
white palaces and landscaped gardens. Then
the younger one found riches of estate
nothing compared with flight's wild timelessness,
ignored the warning, soared to grasp the sun,
and ah! a melting shuttlecock,
fell to the sea's clutch as the other flew
to shelter and the loneliness of age.

ON NEUTRAL GROUND

"She can be traced," the agent said, "but it
won't guarantee she'll even see
you, let alone tell
what happened more than twenty
years ago. A meeting can't compel
her to love you or admit

any wrong." But she came: by hired car, and kept
her married name a secret. She couldn't cope
with a baby, she said, when her lover went
to live abroad. She had no hope,
no money, no support, no time for sentiment.
"My husband doesn't know. You must accept

things as they are; there's too much at stake."
They talked a while, found she'd named
her Joyce, not Jane, and they shared
a love of horses—like her sons. When they came
to leave the wine-bar, both smiled slightly, as their
acquaintance ended in an awkward handshake.

PERSEPHONE

Descent begins with chill of mist
hairblown about the troubled face of dawn,
eyes turning to go, turning to rain
as somewhere leaves depart across a field;
begins with failing arms of golden rod;
begins with vegetables' slow
decline; in answer to the voiceless call
begins with going...

Going with dew-damp hands of frost
on foxglove, hollyhock—pale spells of slanted light
on warmless firethorn, on shadows of water;
going with reluctant freckles of ice
among stones and stems in the late afternoon;
going with fuchsia's hanging head, softly
with breathless fern below footfall of snow,
going on to earth's end...

Ends with earth gripped, ends deeper down,
under hushed bulbs and muttering roots;
ends deeper down, where the cypress is sacred,
ends in oblivion, ends beyond Acheron
in hymnals of patience with ruin and gloom;
ends without love at the desolate solstice
burning with darkness, closed in the clasp
of the withered king.

ON READING THE STAFF LISTS AT
SANDBACH HIGH SCHOOL, 1972 – 93

"Most of these names
Are meaningless to me,"
You said
And I agree
That though the lists are bound in red
They hardly mean the same

As Menin Gate
Or Vietnam Wall, where lists
Are used
(An optimist
Might say) as symbols so we choose
—In future—love, not hate.

Although you see
Their routine purposes,
Staff lists
Do not disclose
To you my knowledge which exists
Within this coterie.

The pages show
No sign of private pain
It's true.
They appertain
To basic facts, to who was who.
The names are all you know.

They tell me more
Than who taught Chemistry
Or Art.
A pageantry—
Hope, pride, its counterpart
Grief to unsettle you for sure—

Lives in these leaves
Where people come and go,
Each page
A studio
Where wisdom, love, bereavement, age
Shape what the names achieve.

Their human bridge
Was built across the years
To guide
Each child, to steer
Each one where wondrous things abide
In light's sweet heritage.

SPEEN

Up a lane that summer cycled
nine years after the atom bomb,
after trams and rationing, a boy

seeking the elusive hostel
up the flecked lane, hot, hazy, hedged
by high green, stillness, thyme and sky.

Conscious that all things change, he rode
to his release uphill, into the shimmering atoms,
into his own past, deep into loved and silent England.

THE LIFE AND TIMES OF
MISS RUTH JONES

She died today at 76; no family
to speak of: parents long dead, her brother
killed in action over Germany, her lover
on a beach in Normandy.

It was her heart. Some people feared
it stopped the week the wedding
was called off, seeing her shedding
suddenly all hope as well as tears.

None of those who knew her lived
to see her die. Their children saw
only a harridan. They couldn't guess the war
left her with no alternative

and that she wanted none. Work, yes,
till she retired as company secretary,
but grief came first. No obituary
records the stubborn loneliness

or passion that made her sing
half a century ago. Friendless
she'll go to her grave, unless
unfriendly neighbours do the decent thing.

WAST WATER, NOVEMBER

Empty guest houses falter
at the wood's fringe and edge
uneasily into the chilling gloom.
The last sign of human order
is the track which winds
where superstitions brood
beneath the vast hostility of stone.

At the world's end the lake
writhes, relishes moss, wishes to grip
the few bitter souls gathered on shingle.
Stone hangs in the air or crashes to water.
Fire, prayers, would offer no consolation.
Over dark water a ferryman is rowing.

HOW TO DIE

One doesn't, I suppose, look forward to
a heart attack outside the paper shop
or in a store, when buying underwear. The chop
seems poor reward for all your work, and you
had other things to do. Now, shovelled off the floor
into an ambulance, you're seen no more

and that, they say, is that. Unfair? At least
there'll be a hymn, some flowers and a tear
or two, brass handles on a lovely box. It's queer
how mourners at a funeral feast
will ponder briefly on their own demise
but soon tuck in to sausages and pies.

I'd rather get an arrow in the back
but stagger bravely on until the guy
leading the cavalry arrives and then die
a hero in the barmaid's arms, not pack
it in with dysentery or flu. I'm miles
from wigwams, though, and going west in style

is, on reflection, far too vigorous.
The O.P.'s home, not knowing who you are,
what day it is, or why the *Daily Star*
reads better upside down, is not so hazardous
a way of snuffing it, but takes too long.
Die, if you must, to music and a song!

The pianist comes on Tuesday afternoons
to play the old-tyme favourites. With luck
if something really nasty struck,
it would be nice to perish to *Blue Moon*,
gasping some last request to the tuneful nurse.
Well, being scoffed by crocodiles is worse.

THREE MOMENTS FROM MYTH

(i) A GIRL WATCHES FROM HER WINDOW

the ceremonious ocean roll
against the headland, the wind whip
words *if anything* of love away,
propel the decorated sail
of a mind not to be changed *about me,*
and *made you happy* with such brimming visions
turns, moves *please, please* with lowered eyes
into her darkening room, lit by a flame.

(ii) THROUGH THE WOODED QUIET

he comes to part the quivering lips of leaves
and views her, nude, by a secluded pool:
hair wet, dream of long neck, passion of slender limbs.
She hears at hand the baying of his hounds.
Reflected in the beaded water drops
running down her belly and blue-veined breasts
seconds before the punishment he sees
the sad eyes of an animal with horns.

(iii) "AT LAST THE LIGHT!" HE TURNS AND
SHE, DELAYED

by slippery moss on stone, grows pale:
her form in its thin shift fades to silver
of birch, is etched on the negative
air by leaf-lines of vein and dissolves
as her mind takes root
in succulent clays. From her kingdom
of silence she watches him stare
and then weep at the marks on a waterworn stone.

RYDAL MOUNT
for Karen

Up a steep lane from road to door.
The house is open: a bright, cottage industry
of guide books, portraits, drawings, maps.
The place probably suggests more
comfort in the nineteenth century
than there really was, but in the end,
Karen, you'd have come away with perhaps
a better sense than I could give you of those motley friends.

Down the garden, through the trees
to the summer house. Locked. From the top
of the path, which loses its way through the wood
among gloomy ferns, I can see
Rydal Water glittering and might stop
(out of season) to listen to silence or the blown
rain or language of winds. He said they could
speak of a spirit dwelling in sky and stone.

He's right, I think. There's an awesome mood
among these lakes and hills, not easily
shrugged off or understood. Even so,
your postcard, kept in my copy of *The Prelude*,
brought fun to Lonscale Fell. Breezily
you claimed the lakeland air made you feel "somehow
more like a drink than a poem" eight years ago.
A contrast to your brief message now

from France. Your brother has been found dead, you say,
aged twenty. No one can account
for loss like this or expect you to withstand
"problems in love, work, everything" alone. Yesterday,
as I read Wordsworth's poems at Rydal Mount,
I remembered your postcard. Today I share your tears
as if you were my daughter. Here's my hand
to help you climb the steep lane of the years.

LEDA

When he fastened her hair's brown wave
at her neck and his fanned hands
swept to the first full caress of her breasts
she thought him a god,

bent to his glamorous thrust,
thrilled at the upping and might
of the god's bone and grasp and rode hard,
knowing he was.

Nailed on a feverous field
as dew formed to the late swifts' screams,
she had no words to answer the tremor
her thighs held or the world coming back.

But she knew in a year he had no wings;
only a baby's wail and a wage.
From the kitchen she watches him
trudge down the road to the factory gate.

LINDA, AT TWENTY

She killed herself because her lover died.
Does some impenetrable cosmic plan
    Lie at the heart of this destruction? Can
    Reasons important to a priest provide
        Comfort of any kind?
What her death has done is remind
Me of losses beyond belief, the blind
        Way she flung her bright talk
And her lovely body into the dark.

It's hard to accept all that's left is her
Light-sounding name in a gloomy graveyard,
    That such impetuous, ill-starred
    Action swept her away. I prefer
        To think of her as though
She's walking along the lane and he says, "Hello"
And the light in her eyes and smiles show
        She will never suppress
A sense of fun, nor her love, which is endless.

THE SEARCH

Tools seeking origins gouge out
stones, scrape out from soil a wall, coins, grain,
fish-bone, traces of fire. What
were these men? No sign of their dread
of travel by night or love of song:
only all manner of quaint device
littering land under thistles and dung.

Hoc tempore monasterium
sancti Benedicti a Longobardis
destructum est.[1]

Axe hacked, skull groaned, sword on shield
clashed here, Christ's flame favoured by few.
Trowels cannot ease evil out
of the ground and cure it for good
and what good there is isn't where
a rusted ring was bribe and reward

Đa cōm of mōre   under mist-hleoþum
Grendel gongan   Godes yrre bær [2]

and tales told men to kindle grimness
as they do now seek to strike strangers down
for money or land or fight in the name
of the Lord for the martyr's fame.
Earth-works ooze blood. Where is an end
to wickednesse? Where the comynge of good?

The dig will be done in genes, stars sought,
quarks scoured, the shovel of art fling up
all manner of quaint device
to glint like gold trinkets in spoil,
but nothing, some say, will surpass
the finding of prayer, of thanks for God's love
when He came where His home was the cross.

[1] From the *Anglo-Saxon Chronicle* for the year 596: "At this time Saint Benedict's monastery was destroyed by the Lombards."

[2] From *Beowulf* (lines 710-11): "Then came from the moor under the misty fells Grendel advancing; God's ire he bore."

BARTON-ON-SEA

When we first came
stone steps led down to sand
some thirty years ago.
The baby didn't understand
how to build castles; so her games
stayed where the pebbles were. These she could throw.

Times change, buildings,
people. Only the sea's
the same and pebbles seem
no longer preferable to sand. She's
out there in the dunes, sheltering
from the world's thrown stones in drugs and dreams.

If we had known
she'd make her life on sand,
the misery she'd undergo
traipsing insubstantial land
below deceptive steps of stone,
we'd wish she'd not been born.

That isn't so.

CLOUD OF UNKNOWING

I find hawthorn in blossom
and the scent of peony and phlox
in our sunlit garden become a custom
and cling to things which hint a ripening.
But ripe pears fall and yew trees darken
the deep green lane. Its harvest is age.

The symmetry of standing moorland stones
tells of an ordering of sun and stars,
bleak rock bent to the purpose—
sacrifice, in granite shadows
to secure corn crop or rain,
even the tribe's survival.

But voices from whirlwinds and sky,
ghosts in the dampness of forests,
miraculous lights over a fen or field
are rare now.
Down rows of yews
bell, song, stone crosses
go to a timeless silence.

As each day dawns I go on
with no answer to why we exist
in this spiral of light.
Mountain, river and beating rain outlast us.
And when your plane leaves for America
and the talk is of land management or design,
I think of the Magellanic Clouds
and, as you fly away,
where fruit will fall and yew trees darken the day.

ON LONGFORD HALL

Standing where shaled, cracked steps
lead to a ruined lawn, I stare at the Hall
long a landmark. Tendrils of wire climb
its bolted steel trellis, locks flower
on rusty stems and branches of gate
and the red and white blossoms
of vigorous danger signs
hang higher than aerosols' range.
Terraces creep under moss.
Rain can get in and petals of stone fall.

A way of life gone: the last carriage,
the Rose Queen, the band, the Hall's
treasures neglected or sold. Civic
and evergreen aliens insist
this house is theirs to pull down,
who need no books, whose customs crawl
or go clambering, or for whom
only now matters: the rest
is all talk and can rot
like the children who played in the gardens.

I look at the boarded windows, the splintered roof—
opened deliberately? —the tarmac
furrowed by root and frost, the pillars
flaking. The Hall is clamped
in an outrageous cage and lours
over the park's smashed benches
and their sour messages. It is
as if the past and persons living there
gave out one long tremendous scream
on being blinded, chained, and then dragged down.

Built in 1857, Longford Hall was the home of John Rylands, the wealthy
Manchester businessman and philanthropist. By order of Trafford Borough
Council the Hall, a listed building, was demolished in the Spring of 1995.

JOURNEYING

Surely it won't be down there?
Turn left at the inn and first right
he said, but here are only small
sad caravans and a store which is closed.

On down a deep lane: the nettled banks
brushing the car; grass, dandelions
crowning the broken road, nothing
coming the other way. And then

the soundless opening to heat
and stunning isolation of white sands.
We face the sun across an empty sea:
a lovely genesis, keeping its secret still.

FOR ALICE, NOT YET BORN

Her name and sex known, address and approximate
date of birth, I could fill in a form
if I had to, though she has no character,
is not yet a person in the modern sense.

Nevertheless, she belongs to the present tense,
is quietly miraculous in a way
that is, and is not, unique. Soon
with an international pedigree

she'll be watching the world or be pretty
loud, making her presence known.
Later, the more refined, she'll turn young men's heads
in Paris or Rome. Of course, no one can say

what the future holds, but I pray
merriment fills her days. Let her be modest, bright,
confident, free from malice or loss,
and learn what's best is a generous heart.

May she love ceremony, music, words, art
and, living long in the next century,
find joy in those not so simple things:
blossom, trees, starlight, wind, rain, the sun on the sea.

August , 1994

DRUMMOSSIE MOOR
16th April, 1746

What brought them here was a mixture of things—
politics, for one; clannish manners, lack
of employment, drink. Some were impressed, some
wanted a fight. What they learned had less
to do with honour or ideal king than with terror
and terror's swipe and battery of iron.

Now you can wander the battlefield or rest
in the visitors' centre, where horror means money
and the general *bonhommie* is a far cry
from brains raining on heather.
An acceptable level of scream
by those being bayoneted and cannon
roar forms the background to video stills.

How else could it be? Romantic disguise persists
in that hunt among mountains and mists
and the fresh wind filling tall sails.
Better to dwell on this than consequent
snapping of necks, or being locked in a barn
and burned. Such fashionable policies
came out of rooms hushed by tapestries,
while banquets in Rome continued for forty-two years.

THE OLD ZOO

A pity it has to close.
The fact is nobody goes
there these days, not in vast
numbers anyway. It's too
caged in. It's expensive to run. Last
week there were only a few

keepers left, packing baffled small
mammals in crates, shutting each lid
on rustle of straw, call
for release and wide timid
eyes. A man with fists that could kill
lowers a bird with a big orange bill

into a box and tries to hide
a mark that's splashed its cardboard side.
Men coaxing Josie the elephant
into the lorry's steel cube make slow
dangerous progress. She doesn't want
to go, doesn't seem to know

she's part of a conservation
plan at a new destination
or that the ramp and these chains
are for her own good. A blinking lizard
and querulous parrots with limited brains
are puzzled, too. They think it a hazard.

All of which shows they're the same
as us, more or less. Ferrets, kestrels, cats could claim
zoos are cruel, I suppose, but a sort of trust
has grown between them and the men
who feed them and keep them clean and who must
have been equally baffled when

news of the closing-down came through.
Take the chap with the biceps who cried.
Not that he's lost his job. The zoo
is his life, its chirps and purrings his pride,
without which it's easy to see who'll
suffer most from the closure and find it cruel.

THE CLAY PIT

Nearly fifty years ago my crazy raft
swamped and abandoned, I sank in grey
lifeless water, then into clay, as I
struggled to land, grasping
the pole in a friend's hand and pulled
towards gravel and eight-year-old
promise never to go there again.
A little later on we said our prayers
at school with hands together and
eyes closed when Arthur Lindsay drowned.

With an hour to kill I broke my promise
yesterday and drove to that deep depressing
scoop, casually thinking I'd discover
Arthur, feel his spirit drift
among thin reeds, bike frames and cans
buried by rosebay willowherb,
or catch his ghost sailing a piece of fence
roped to a yellow door. I found the clay pit
filled and grassed to make a playing-field
where men and women walk their dogs.

PIAZZA DI SPAGNA 26, ROMA

This room is where he died:
the fireplace original,
a door walled up. At his death all
furniture was burned. A death mask, pages
of manuscript and drawings now provide
relics for callers to revivify
in wood-framed, glass sarcophagi
his rasping breath, agony and rage.

A cosmopolitan, summer crowd
outside. In here a studied stillness,
as if afraid of illness,
and talk that's not too loud.
Then down the stairs
out into the chattering, languid air.

He faced an enemy in those last days
which doesn't care for weeping, being brave,
faith or the lack of it, but a grave
isn't all the earth possesses
after his fever and fret. He's always
there by the lake's withered sedge, or in the shade
of warm trees, and—yes! —crossing a moonlit glade
to greet enchantment's gods and goddesses.

EDWARD THOMAS IN HAMPSHIRE

Wych-elms, white of anemone and wood-
pigeon cooing consoled him,
but his Eden of sunned tile
and thatch was drifting
away. Among wood-smoke and fallen
apples the thudding of guns.

From Froxfield through harebells and gorse
he sought whatever it was he knew
he would never hold: like a wren's
intuition, time, England. Alone,
often in heavy rain, he strode
over hill-ridge and fields, his mind
an owl cry, tormented by things
that are nameless or have no end.

FOREST CHAPEL

Not much to see. The place we didn't plan on
bare and plain: some sturdy pews,
whitewashed walls, a memorable date or two,
the three kings' window. Bearing no gifts,
we bought a pamphlet, slightly damp.

Outside: the graveyard and a brief search
for lime-green lady's mantle and sweet
cicely, the pamphlet's herbs. You scratched
a coverlet of matted grass to make sense
of a stone. The death remained unknown.

Back to the gate with its low wall,
a spot for ramblers to kneel,
unpack their sandwiches and open cans.
Next door a bye-law poster sought to turn
their right of way around, not through, the farm.

Three accidental pilgrims, we drove on down.
But as the sun swept Wildboarclough
and the hills lifted the chapel and graves to the light
I thought no hand can scratch
and get at the truth of this, or that.

ISLANDS

Here granite bison dance
above the flickering. Later
sounds are written down.

And here at dawn
comes joy of the Lord,
toil in the summer fields.

Here sophisticated prows slice sand,
heroes of the kill are crowned,
rings and promises exchanged.

And here the Moon, where no green
grows and Mars, where no gentle hands
pledge love or praise the stars.

KOBE, 1995
for Harry Guest

Their son in rubble
and dusty air dead,
the couple light candles,
place lotus root, wine
and rice at their shrine
for his lone after-life.
He was unmarried.

They wish him to wed
one who suffered the same
toppling rock and flame
for family sake.

Prayer brings a slender girl
stepping on willow
leaves. Her gold bangles
shine like a vow, like tears
in eyes that revere
the rising of light.
The son takes her hand.

LATELY DEAD

"...it was as if, lately dead, she heard the living talking."
Night and Day, Virginia Woolf

Each room continues to be functional, though she died
so unexpectedly: noise of water, plates and tea-
cups chinking, the telephone bell, someone opening a door,
crying, saying how talented and beautiful she was,
things like that. Like that holiday in Cornwall
when the lilac was coming into bloom, remember?
She sang *Pale Hands I Loved beside the Shalimar*
and we danced at nightfall to ragtime jazz on the lawn.

Turn from this weeping and talk, Katharine.
Life goes on, they say.

Though I am here, where fresh irises
bloom in the cool hall, in the drawing-room though I am
        there
voices are where I am lilac at nightfall, and song,
far away, as if they, as if I, someone, turned
on a stair and stopped, amazed, seeing the arrowed geese
dark in the window above the lake, where I bathe and fade
and my tears fall into shadows, though I have no eyes
and will not speak and am no more moved by their
        speaking, now,
as I remember the drawing-room and drift from the stair
and the hall into thinned weeping and words in air, into
        thin air.

OEDIPUS AT COLONUS

Finally, the signs came: sky fire, thunder,
meteors flashing, showering
his mind's element. He knew what gods
could do and made them offerings.

Those who returned from the Brazen Stair
spoke of tears, libations, absence
of pain, but that was all. Only
Theseus saw, if he saw, the Kindly Ones
but wouldn't say what happened or where.

So what began with a riddle ended in one:
sunlight piercing the green glade,
water, voices calling and singing
and a group of people being turned away
from a vanishing not properly accounted for
to face their own blind change to silence, to earth.

THE BRIDGEWATER CANAL

Frantic once with crates crashing, money, muck,
when barge-horses strained to tow coal mostly
and crowds of rough-clothed hard men cursed their luck
like a snapped ratchet, it's now ghostly,
lacks shouts about pulleys and rates of pay,
pots, china too fragile to go by road
or any miscellaneous cartload
stacked in the dingy yards: Staffordshire clay,

sacks of grain, iron, salt. Its dead flat miles
are edged by jobless fishermen, who sit
glued to the overcast afternoon, while
a dog yawns and impatient sparrows flit
past broken-windowed warehouses, mills, cranes.
The water laps these disappointed places,
consumes bikes, prams, dropped spanners, necklaces,
flushes the grease from chip wrappers and drains,

or, strangely shadowed where the last bridge bends
to each green bank and tall field grasses
unravel silence as it descends
again after a narrow boat passes,
makes weekend skippers worship peace of a kind
like ripples on brickwork, a waving sky
and shapes too vague to identify
dancing, like lives, out of sight, out of mind.

A LATE FLOWERING

You see them occasionally, solemn
families in polished limousines
(the chauffeur and his calm companion
silenced behind glass) taking a clean,
soft, gently purring ride in black;
what talk there is—subdued,
confined to platitudes
about the one who isn't coming back.

Flesh, started with a slap and a loud
cry in a green-walled room, washed, weighed
and cuddled up to mum, ends in a shroud
of cellophaned flowers and ribbons. Dismayed,
unpractised voices lift in song, desire
their supplications soar
beyond arched stone before
the curtained vestibule of fire.

One thinks of it, gone: ill or well spent;
certainly not of kaleidoscopic fungi
turning tree stumps into something different—
white, crimson, yellow, brown as they putrefy.
Yet here is a similar integument
of sprays and wreaths. The hearse
swings through gates. We traverse
our own paths to this grave event.

SARAH, TRAVELLING

Driving from Belle Vue home, I saw—
was it? — that girl I passed in a flash—
my daughter, her hair dropping over her face,
a heavy bag slung over her bowed shoulder?

I braked, but missed the turn and then went on.
Six years too late. No going back
to embarrass a stranger or find again
heroin's persistent point in Sarah's eyes.

In late October sunshine
students, walking to restaurants or pubs
or a park with friends, were talking
of love, no doubt, and politics
and beer and what our purpose is
in being here. Each fair, vivacious girl recalled
my daughter heading for the hostel's homeless rooms.

Unsettled, yes, those last few miles.
Then I reached home. And there
instead of family and friends we share
abandoned things: books, pictures, tapes,
a teddy bear. This empty car.

FUGITIVES

"Rapt, twirling in thy hand a wither'd spray,
And waiting for the spark from heaven to fall."
The Scholar-Gipsy, Matthew Arnold

From a pear-tree's shade, where the lawn
drifts to spent lilac and laburnum, I hear hot broom
crack and water fall to the pond and, beyond,
the motorway's dim humming. Home
on the rim of this north-west centre of trade
and industry and hooting trams is the place,
if anywhere, to recover hope or at least
some sense of the ideal the Scholar-Gipsy has—
who we must imagine exempt from age
and rarely seen round here: wandering once
by the river Dane; in dappled
Delamere one summer evening, or
battling against the snow on the moor
above Macclesfield, striding towards
a hill where the true light might finally
break out far more spectacularly
than that other bright fugitive of ice and gas
crossing the constellations, its incandescent
head and tail sewn into chronicles, equally
at home in the future as in the past.

LES PENDUS DE MONTFAUCON, 1493

Their hands are tied, their faces pained,
mildly surprised, or looking sleepy like
the man with a beard. All five could be standing
on grass, but they're not. The heavy cross-
beam easily takes their weight.
Time is at their disposal.

The moment the world gave way they bumped,
wriggled together, with no inclination to see
how the others were getting on or take in
the crowd's cheap roar. Now they are perfectly still,
resigned to waiting for crows, then flies.
A few feet below is a skull, plus two bones
and a horseshoe, added for special
effects. It seems a dear price to pay
for putting a foot in the lord's own forest
or stealing a loaf of bread or a lamb.

Five hundred years later these figures
(four in faded blue smocks and one
who's forgotten or lost his shirt)
would be bemused by the fame
wood and strong ropes have brought them. They can be
      found
on the cover of François Villon's *Selected Poems*,
published by Penguin at £6.99.
That's cheap for some, for others dear.

SHELLEY...

was always spectacular
and on the razzle or make, or move,
till he failed to return to the house
with the sea beneath windows. Here at Lerici,
pacing the terrace above the swell
in a mood, he met his own ghost and was
questioned on happiness.

Often deranged, he was both terrorist
and martyr: church, state, wedlock enough
to set him stamping and unleash
apparitions and screams.
Harriet called him a vampire.

Unable to quell in his electric senses
a need to investigate beauty and terror,
he refused an instruction to reef his sails
and compelled himself to a battle with frantic water.
Into the Gulf of Spezia, under full sail,
he went down, confounding his stormed
brain's wizardry and thunderflash.

What washed to the shore
in ten days' time could have been anyone
except for the nankeen trousers and white silk socks,
Leigh Hunt's copy of *Keats* in a pocket—
the face completely eaten away,
arms bitten by curious fish.

On a sun-stung beach near Viareggio
Byron, Trelawny, Hunt and some
Tuscan militia and fishermen
witnessed his body burn,
crackle in an iron cradle, seethe, spit
and spark like his poems — rebels
and chemistry, monsters, alchemy
(tameless, and swift, and proud)
drifting high and wide in the air over the deep blue bay.

ON NATIONAL SERVICE

In 1957 I met a man
in a large, army shed in the south of England.
His job was to bash out dents
in ammunition boxes, scrape
rust with a wire brush and send
clean boxes clattering across
the conversation of gravity runway
for new applications of paint.

A former army major in Hungary,
he was a lawyer till in '56
he escaped from the Russians with only his language.
His English was unimpressive like his
standard issue grey denim overalls.
He couldn't be a lawyer here.

Did he go back? I don't know,
but I've thought of him over
the long boredom of time and trust
he did. His gloved hands caught slivers
of hope, hammered out freedom
with a wooden mallet and shut steel hasps
on the boxes he filled with anger and sorrow.

PERSUASION

Call love into question
if loving her lips' red might mean
at the first apple bite
some terrifying deity
springs from behind a cloud
to usher in woe.

For wherever lovers go
unparadised, far from a crowd,
one's cute velleity
is most unlikely to excite
the other, unless she's been
open to suggestion.

HILL FARMER

On the land's surge towards lark song
he tries to hold sway. The moment
light hits the curtains
he goes to stack stones in a wall.
His mind is bound to the silence of turf,
to the wall, to crow-caw and leaning thorns
where a brief wind spins wool ;
and where a field drain
empties across the choked ditch
his boots suck up mud.
He'll clear it after he's checked his sheep.

When the sun blazes
behind the stunted trees on the hill
he turns for home.

In the long silences his wife
sips steaming tea and, hunched,
looks forward to market day.
He broods by the ticking clock
on the cost of a broken gate.
Clenched against favours and winter
they serve the imperative land.

TO A BLACKBIRD

You've been at it all afternoon,
ripping out moss among
the pond's marsh marigolds. You hop
on rocks, then fly back,
but knowing the neighbourhood
don't go straight home. You take steps:
the fence, the cherry tree, are stops
to deceive cats, magpies, me, until
you vanish into Barbara's conifer.

Your beak's green fronds will soften
the earlier wickerwork. Skilled
in upholstery, did
you and your mate agree
on the carpet's colour, on matching cushions?
Such a plush lining
of intricate wispy twigs may be
a sign of instinctive good taste,
but I think much more is built
into your house and mine: that warmth
which sustains our fragile clinging-on.